Guiding Lights

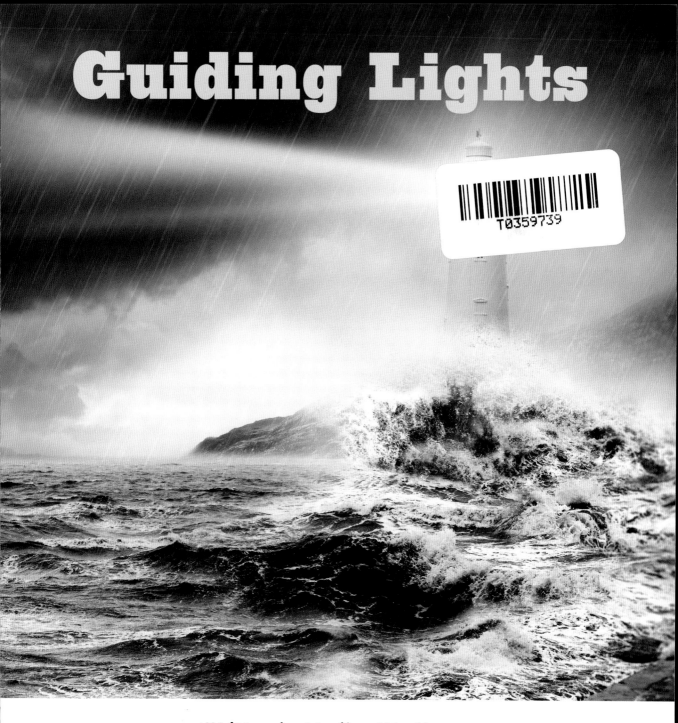

Written by Marilyn Woolley
Series Consultant: Linda Hoyt

WorldWise
Content-based Learning

Contents

Introduction

From ancient times, sailors set out in wooden sailing ships carrying goods and people to foreign ports and, in doing so, they faced great dangers.

Storms blew without warning, bringing gale-force winds of 112 kilometres per hour or more, and huge rolling waves up to seven metres high throwing up spouts of spray. Thick fog and sleet also made visibility difficult, particularly at night.

As a result, many ships sailing near coastlines crashed into or were blown against rugged, rocky cliffs, ledges and submerged reefs. These ships often broke up and sank to the bottom of the ocean. This loss of ships, their **cargo** and the people on them became an increasing problem, especially as trade between countries increased, and more ships made long journeys to foreign ports.

A strong clear light that could be seen by sailors when they were still far away from danger was needed.

But for hundreds of years it was not possible to create such a light, although many solutions were tried and gradual improvements were made. Ships continued to sink, cargo was lost, and sailors and passengers died.

Early lighthouses

The oldest aid to **navigation** is the lighthouse. A lighthouse is a high tower with a light on top. Built on or near the water's shoreline, lighthouses are meant to guide ships in dangerous waters as they come near land.

First lighthouses

The first lighthouse dates back to the days of ancient Egypt. Although it was no more than a bonfire on top of a hill, it served the same purpose as lighthouses do today – it warned ships of dangerous hazards.

From the days of the Roman Empire until the 1700s, lighthouses did not change very much. They were basically stone towers with fires burning at the top.

The first **authenticated** lighthouse tower structure was the Pharos of Alexandria. It was built on the island of Pharos in 300 BCE. Between 117 metres and 134 metres tall, it was among the tallest man-made structures on the earth for many centuries, and known as one of the seven wonders of the ancient world.

The Romans built lighthouse towers in Ostia in 50 BCE at the mouth of the Tiber River. They allowed safe passage to Rome. This lighthouse appears on coins and historical artwork.

A painting of the Lanterna of Genoa. This lighthouse was built on the Mediterranean coast of modern-day Genoa in 1128, and wood was burned to make a flame as a guiding light.

Early lighthouses in Europe

As travel by ship and the trade of goods between European countries increased in the centuries up to the 1700s, many more lighthouses were built along the coastlines of Britain and other countries across Europe.

In 1699, a wooden tower was built in the open sea off Plymouth, England. This was the Eddystone Lighthouse, and the first lighthouse to be built in Britain. The foundation of this high wooden tower was **cemented** onto rock.

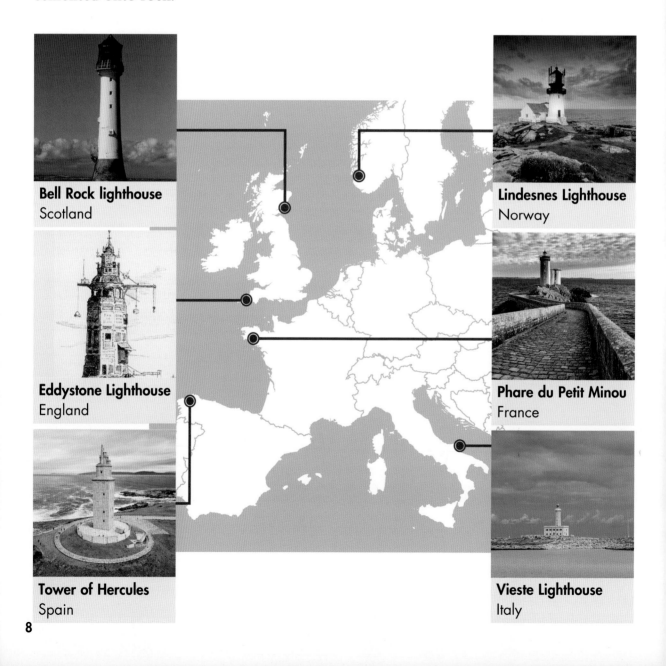

Bell Rock lighthouse
Scotland

Eddystone Lighthouse
England

Tower of Hercules
Spain

Lindesnes Lighthouse
Norway

Phare du Petit Minou
France

Vieste Lighthouse
Italy

The oldest existing rock lighthouse in the British Isles is the Bell Rock lighthouse, built on a dangerous reef in the North Sea off the coast of Scotland.

It was difficult to construct, because the rock on which it was built is above water only at low tide, and when the tide is high, the rock is five metres underwater.

Work began in 1807, and it was not finished until 1811. But the lighthouse is still in use today!

Early lighthouses in the British colonies

In the 1600s, the British established a colony in North America. During this time, they sent shiploads of convicts across the ocean to their new colony.

As contact and trade between Europe and North America grew, many more lighthouses were needed. The first lighthouse in North America was built in 1716, on Little Brewster Island off Boston Harbor.

In 1776, the Americans won the War of Independence against the British. The British could no longer send their convicts to North America. They needed another penal colony, and soon found one at Port Jackson, in Australia.

Little Brewster Island with Boston Light

Early lighthouses in Australia

In 1788, 11 British sailing ships carrying soldiers and convicts arrived at Port Jackson. They raised the British flag and declared Port Jackson a British colony. More convict ships soon followed.

To keep the ships safe, a beacon light was built in 1793 on the south head of Sydney Harbour. It was fired by coal and wood, and kept alight by convicts. It was replaced with the Macquarie Lighthouse in 1818.

The main penal colony, however, was in Van Diemen's Land (Tasmania). To help guide ships to Hobart, a lighthouse was built in 1833 at Iron Pot, a small island in the mouth of the Derwent River.

Over the next 200 years, more than 350 Australian lighthouses were built around Australia's coastline, which is 37,000 kilometres long. Hazards for ships sailing to Australia included rough seas, rocks, reefs and gale-force winds.

Did you know?
Between 1788 and 1868, more than 168,000 British convicts were sent to Australia by ship. Many other people migrated to Australia, and thousands lost their lives in shipwrecks.

The first lighthouse in Sydney, the Macquarie Lighthouse. This stone lighthouse was powered by whale oil.

The Iron Pot Lighthouse at the entrance to the Derwent River, Tasmania

The problem of the light

From the days of the first bonfire on the hill in ancient Egypt, people knew that they needed more effective warning lights.

Burning fires

Coal, wood, fires, braziers   Up to 1850

Early warning lights consisted of open fires. Later, iron baskets known as braziers were used. They were often unreliable and either burned with lots of flame –and therefore light, which could be dangerous – or too little flame with lots of smoke, which obscured the light.

Old Isle of May lighthouse with burning brazier

In the 18th and 19th centuries, engineers struggled with the problem of how to make the light stronger and clearer so that it could be seen far out at sea. But development depended on the technology and knowledge available at the time. Progress was slow.

Candles   1540–1790

Candles were used in many lighthouses in the 1500s. The light from individual candles was **feeble**, but when a number of candles were used together the light was stronger than the light generated by fires.

While the candles provided more consistent light, they constantly needed replacing. They were expensive, and they were also very smelly.

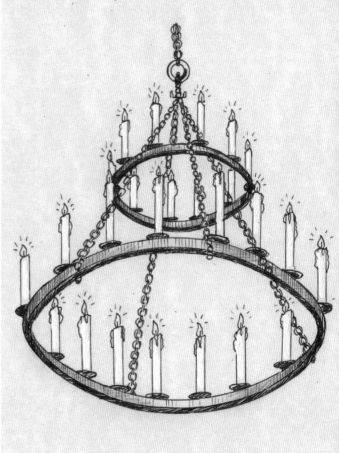

The candelabra originally installed in Eddystone Lighthouse, in 1759.

13

Gradual improvements: Lamps 1500–1910

The earliest forms of oil lamps consisted of stone bowls filled with oil and one or more small rope wicks. They produced poor light with much smoke and fumes. Initially, fish oil and seal oil were burned in these lamps and, later, whale oil.

A smokeless lamp   1782

Swiss scientist Aime Argand invented an oil lamp that did not create smoke so the light could be seen clearly.

The lamp had a circular wick with a glass chimney. This provided a current of air, which kept the oil burning evenly.

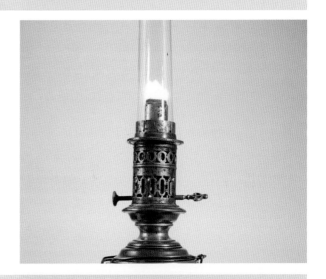

A stronger light   1901

Arthur Kitson and David Hood replaced oil with kerosene to power the light. The light was six times stronger than the light from oil-wick lamps.

Gas lamps

A flashing gas light

Gustaf Dalén used a gas to produce
a flashing light that could be left
unattended. Gas automatically lit the
light at nightfall and **extinguished** it at
sunrise. The lighthouse keeper no longer
had to watch the lamp and less gas was
needed to keep the flame alight.

Gustaf Dalén

The Fresnel lens

Light from many directions

For many years, people tried to increase the power of the light by putting mirrors behind the flame, and placing magnifying glasses in front of the flame. These methods had little effect, and the light still could not be seen for more than a few kilometres, even on a clear night. During stormy weather, the light might be visible for less than one and a half kilometres. In the days of sailing ships, often the light was seen too late and the ship became wrecked on the rocks.

But at last a solution to this problem was found in 1822. Of all the inventions, the Fresnel lens has had the most significant impact on the way light in lighthouses was created. The invention changed the way light in lighthouses was projected.

If a candle or a lamp is sitting on a table, the light spreads out evenly and shines in all directions. This is good if you want to light a whole room, but not useful if you want a long, powerful beam of light.

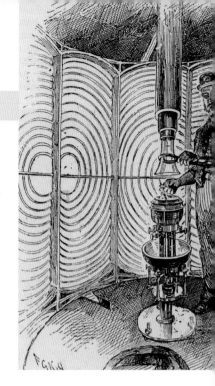

Augustin-Jean Fresnel

Find out more

The amazing curved Fresnel lenses are still in use around the world today. Find out where Fresnel lenses are still being used – you may be interested to hear that car headlamps are one of the places you will find them.

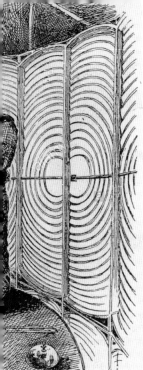

Augustin-Jean Fresnel, a French scientist, discovered a way to increase the strength of the light. He constructed a lens made of specially and focused the light from a flame into a strong, narrow beam. This light could be seen from a distance of just over 30 kilometres.

Today, many of Fresnel's lenses, manufactured over a century ago, guide ships through the night.

Chapter 3

How were lighthouses constructed?

Because they were built in remote or difficult places, early lighthouses were constructed of materials that were close at hand – wood or stones. Those built of wood were at risk of fire.

Towers made from stones were built by simply piling one stone on top of another, and holding them together with **mortar**. They were not as strong as later designs made from specially cut stone blocks that fitted together smoothly.

This cylindrical, stone lighthouse was built in 1848 on the cliffs high above the treacherous Southern Ocean.

Designs of these early lighthouses were based on the principle that towers need a large base that then tapered towards the top. The base provided support for the tower.

Some of the lighthouses were built on land close to the sea, and while the weather conditions were harsh, they were protected from wave damage.

But others were built on rocks in the water and in stormy weather were at risk of damage from strong waves. Eventually, towers were designed with gently curving sides so that when strong waves reached the walls, these waves followed the curve and flowed up the sides of the tower. The force of the waves was not so strong and there was less damage to the tower.

Sunrise at Byron Bay Lighthouse, which is on the most easterly point in Australia.

How the design of lighthouses changed over time

The Eddystone lighthouses

Eddystone is probably the most famous of all lighthouses in England. The various versions show very clearly how the design of lighthouses developed as more information about good design became available.

The Eddystone Lighthouses 1698–1882

Eddystone Lighthouse Numbers 1 and 2

Winstanley, 1698–1699

Eddystone Lighthouse Number 3

Rudyerd, 1709

The first Eddystone Lighthouse was built by Henry Winstanley and was constructed of wood. It suffered heavy weather damage and had to be rebuilt the following spring.

This second lighthouse lasted for four years until 1703, when England was hit by a violent hurricane that swept away the lighthouse. The lighthouse keepers were drowned, as was Winstanley, who was visiting at the time.

These early lighthouses were highly decorative with many features – they look unusual!

This lighthouse was a much less decorative and streamlined tower, with a solid base of stones. The tower was made of timber planks, sealed and made watertight, and it lasted for 47 years until it burned down. The candles in the lantern that produced the light set fire to the roof. The fire burned for five days and completely destroyed the tower.

Think about ...
Why does a lighthouse have a spiral staircase?

Eddystone Lighthouse Number 4

Smeaton, 1759

Eddystone Lighthouse Number 5

Douglass, 1882

The designer of the fourth Eddystone Lighthouse was John Smeaton. He used the very best of new design **principles**. The lighthouse was built of blocks of granite, securely fitted together and sealed with a quick drying cement that he invented himself. It became the accepted standard for lighthouses worldwide.

This tower lasted for 17 years until the rock it was built on started to crumble and a new tower had to be built. The local citizens valued it so much that money was raised to dismantle the tower and to rebuild it on land in Plymouth, where it stands today.

The current tower, completed in 1882 and designed by James Douglass, is the largest tower to be built on the reef, standing almost 30 metres above sea level.

During the last 60–70 years, a number of changes have been introduced to the tower. The lighthouse is still in use today, and the beam can be seen up to 27 kilometres away.

The lighthouse keepers

The keeper of the light

The life of a lighthouse keeper has fascinated people for centuries.

It was a busy life. Keepers were required to fill out a daily logbook recording work done, events, shipping traffic and weather conditions. These logbooks record the range of duties and the strict routine that had to be followed if the light was to shine out each night.

The job was busy and it could also be dangerous. There were many ways keepers could injure themselves while going about routine tasks. Painting the outside of the tower was a particularly dangerous job, and in such an isolated spot, medical help was far away.

Lighthouses are always built in or near dangerous waters. In heavy fog, ships could run **aground** on rocks, and many lighthouse keepers risked their lives trying to rescue crew and passengers from sinking ships.

Fire was a constant danger. Until more modern times, all lamps burned some form of oil or kerosene. In fact, fire or falling were the two greatest hazards to the keepers.

How would you describe the life of a lighthouse keeper – and his family. Busy? Boring? Dangerous? Lonely?

Most lighthouse keepers would not have traded jobs with anyone else.

The logbook of a lighthouse keeper

A lighthouse keeper had to clean the lens and the lantern room so that the light would shine as brightly as possible.

7pm: At sunset, climb the stairs to light the lamp.

8pm–5am: Check the light during the night. (If there was a clock with a system of weights that drove the rotating lenses, a keeper would wind this clock up every two hours to keep the lenses turning.) Read or write notes about their work.

5.30am: At sunrise, climb the stairs to extinguish the lamp.

5.45am: Trim the burned wick of the lamp to try to stop it causing smoke and dirtying the lens.

6am: Clean the lens and lantern room.

7–11am: Rest or sleep.

3–6pm: Carry out any repair jobs. Paint or whitewash the outside walls to keep the lighthouse tower highly visible to any passing ship.

Unload food supplies or new equipment from delivery boats. Write up tasks and new orders.

CASE STUDY | Fay Howe: The lighthouse messenger girl

Fay Howe was born in 1899. She grew up on Breaksea Island, near Albany, Western Australia. Her father was the lighthouse keeper at Breaksea Island Lighthouse.

Growing up on this remote island, Fay was not able to go to school, but her parents taught her to read and write. They also taught her how to send signals with flags, semaphore, Morse code and telegrams. Many people were to benefit from these communication skills.

In 1915, during World War I, thousands of Australian and New Zealand troops gathered in Albany to travel overseas by ship to Egypt and Europe. From the lighthouse on Breaksea Island, Fay used semaphore flags and Morse code to convey messages between these young men and their families.

Fay continued to send family messages to these soldiers as they fought in Egypt and Gallipoli. When she received replies from these homesick soldiers, she used Morse code to relay these messages to Albany. From Albany these messages were sent around the country, printed as telegrams and delivered to families and friends.

BREAKSEA ISLAND.—West Australia.

Fay became a wartime hero. A book, *The Lighthouse Girl* by Dianne Wolfer, tells the story of Fay's remarkable wartime effort.

A sketch of the Breaksea Island Lighthouse, 1863

Breaksea Island in King George Sound, Western Australia

Remote and alone

In 1914, when Fay was 15 years old, her mother died. If the weather was bad and the supply boat did not come, Fay caught rabbits and muttonbirds, and gathered nettles so she and her father had food to eat.

▼ Transports with first Australian and New Zealand expeditionary forces, lying in King George's Sound, WA, 31 October 1914

Chapter 5

The introduction of electric lights

In the late 19th century, the use of electric lamps became more common in lighthouses.

In most lighthouses today, lighthouse keepers are no longer needed to maintain the lights. Electric lighting systems and motors that drive the equipment and lenses have been installed. Diesel or solar-powered batteries often assist the electricity supplied to lighthouses.

This means that the flashing patterns and signals from the lighthouse are automated so a keeper is not needed. People now work in lighthouse control centres and use telephone, radio or satellite systems to check the function of most lighthouses.

The Statue of Liberty: A working lighthouse

The Statue of Liberty was designed and constructed in France by sculptor Frédéric-Auguste Bartholdi and built by Gustave Eiffel (who later designed the Eiffel Tower in Paris) to commemorate the centennial of the American War of Independence.

In 1886, the Statue of Liberty became a working lighthouse to aid ships entering New York Harbor. Its 110-metre-high torch was lit by an arc of nine electric lamps that beamed to ships up to 38 kilometres away, or so it was claimed.

Although the Lighthouse Board attempted to upgrade the lighting system in the torch over the years, the statue's design made for a poor lighthouse, and it remained nearly invisible at night.

The Statue of Liberty was officially discontinued as an aid to navigation on 1 March 1902.

Although the Statue of Liberty was almost useless as a lighthouse, it quickly became a landmark that defined the New York City skyline.

Other navigational signals

There are many other navigational aids besides lighthouses. Lightships, for example, are floating lighthouses. The first Australian lightship was used in Sydney Harbour in 1836.

Recently, new technologies have almost eliminated the need for lightships. Tower structures and buoys have replaced lightships.

Buoys are floating containers that have anchors to keep them in place. They mark the highways of the sea, much the way lines painted on roads tell you where the centre and soft shoulders are.

A navigational lighting buoy, Sydney Harbour, Australia

The newest aid to navigation is electronics. Beams of energy are emitted from a shore station, and equipment on board a ship can measure the beam and work out how far away the ship is from that station. Since the precise location of the station is known, the equipment on the ship can identify the ship's location. These electronic aids are called LORAN and OMEGA, and they guide the ship when it is far out at sea.

Today, there is a network of about 500 visual and electronic aids to navigation at hundreds of sites around Australia's coastline.

The Australian Maritime Safety Authority (AMSA) coordinates the system, which includes lighthouses, beacons, buoys and Global Positioning Systems (GPSs).

Above: A lightship
Left: Electronic navigation on board a ship

This buoy has instruments that measure and record data such as sea surface temperature, air temperature, air pressure, wave height, storm surge, wind speed and rainfall.

Conclusion

Throughout history, people have invented ways to use lights on land to guide ships as they come near coastlines and ports. These lights tell ships of their position in the ocean, warn them of dangerous hazards and assist them in stormy or foggy weather.

New inventions and technology have meant that the nature of these lights, and the lighthouse towers that contain them, has changed over time. But lighthouses are still an important tool in communicating different patterns of flashing lights to help ships safely navigate around the coastlines and harbours of the world.

Glossary

aground   stuck on the ground

authenticated   proven real and genuine

cargo   something that is carried from one place to another by ship

cemented   held together with cement

extinguished   to cause something to stop burning

feeble   very weak

mortar   a wet substance that holds things, such as stones, together

navigation   the act of finding a way to get to a place when travelling

principles   laws or facts of nature that explain how something works or why something happens

steamships   ships powered by steam

Index